# TRIATHLETE MINDSET

*Aspire to Redefine What's Possible for You*

By Morgon Latimore

**Triathlete Mindset**

*Aspire to Redefine What's Possible for You*

Cover Design & Interior Layout by Nicole Wurtele
Cover photo and author's bio photo by Ken Oots

All photos courtesy of Morgon Latimore unless otherwise noted.

**Published by CG Sports Publishing**

A Division of The CG Sports Company
Cejih Yung, CEO and Founder
www.cgsportsco.com

ISBN: 978-1-7359193-7-9

Quantity order requests can be emailed to:
Publishing@cgsportsmanagement.com

Printed in The United States of America

# ENDORSEMENTS

"*Triathlete Mindset* transcends the sport into a way of thinking and living. Through Coach Morgon's explanations of training for a triathlon, we are able to discover more of what is underneath the surface in our everyday life to overcome fears, manage expectations, and overcome struggles. After reading it, I am filled with gratitude for this book and would recommend it to anyone looking to get into triathlon or a way to get motivated to take on life in a new perspective." – *Leo Manzano, two-time Olympian*

"*Triathlete Mindset* is a resource for beginner and experienced athletes alike. This book is loaded with real-world examples of processes to help triathletes accomplish their goals in and out of the sport." – *Mark Goddard, Zoot Sport marketing director*

"Morgon Latimore is truly The Peoples Coach! Insightful, powerful, encouraging! Morgan's easy and understandable approach to triathlon and Ironman training is a breath of fresh air in a sport that is oftentimes intimidating for the everyday man or woman." – *Conway Bowman, outdoorsman, co-host of the "The Outfitters"*

# TABLE OF CONTENTS

# FOREWORD

True success in triathlon is more finesse than fitness, more cerebral than physical, more soulful than sheer strength. *Triathlete Mindset*, Coach Morgon's fourth book, explores these winning qualities and gets to the heart of what makes a true triathlete tick.

He also challenges the conventional idea of who and what is a "true" triathlete. In reading this book, you'll learn that it's not always the person who crosses the line first or the one who lines up eagerly at the start, jumping with excitement at the gun. More often, it's the regular person who seeks a challenge and finds it in the middle or back of the pack.

Stories of regular people who are extraordinary athletes fill the pages of *Triathlete Mindset,* giving us a glimpse into what it takes to get the most out of our own triathlete journeys. Coach Morgon introduces a key triathlon value in each chapter, and he uses his own experiences, plus his own athletes, to illustrate those values in action.

Anyone who knows Coach Morgon like I do – personally, professionally, or even just through his social media accounts – knows that he tells it like it is. He's not one to gloss over something to be nice or to make anyone feel better. At the same time, he overflows with empathy and erupts with energy. The combination of his straight talk, heartfelt care, and motivational mojo is what makes him stand out and above in a sea of coaches and among men. It's also why *Triathlete Mindset* is such a powerful addition to any triathlete's library and why I consider it my privilege to contribute to it.

In this book, you'll learn about vulnerability and how honesty with yourself and openness with others can propel you through your hardest workouts and races. You'll read how friendships and partners serve to motivate and hold you accountable. You'll dig deep into some dark places, and learn how that lights the way to your strongest days. Coach Morgon's personal insights and his athletes' testimonies will resonate and be relatable, and you'll find yourself both reflecting and trying to mirror their examples.

The stories in *Triathlete Mindset* will speak to you, and if you listen, you will hear them cheering for you not only to cross the finish line first but to start in the first place – to aspire to redefine what's possible for you. They will help you find your own voice in triathlon and all aspects of your life.

Read. Reflect. Enjoy. And love the lessons in *Triathlon Mindset*. No doubt, you'll find yourself applying what you learn well beyond race day.

– Holly Neumann

# INTRODUCTION

When I started writing this book, I thought it would be for the beginner triathlete. I wanted to help answer all the questions and insecurities new people might have about not just the practical aspects of triathlon but the culture and mindset, as well.

This is that book. But it's also more.

As I wrote, and as I talked to others about the topics covered in the book, I realized how many veteran triathletes also needed the reminders, reinforcements, encouragement, and support that this book covers.

So if you're curious about what it takes to get started in triathlon, and you're also looking for real-life tips and inspiration, you're in the right place. And if you're someone who's been around awhile and wants to dig deeper into what makes triathletes great, you're in the right place, too.

In this book, we'll talk about what traits make a person successful in triathlon, so you can prepare to be your best. You'll learn how to push through doubt, gain confidence, and enjoy the triathlon journey.

We'll cover topics that illustrate what I consider to be triathlon's core values – perseverance, encouragement, adventure, community, enthusiasm, vulnerability, value, peace, mindfulness, and voice. You'll be well-versed in all these things before the end of this book.

There's no reason to delay, and knowledge is a huge

confidence-booster, so let's jump in with some triathlon Q&A and a little pep talk.

*Why triathlon?*

As people get older, many choose to do individual sports over team sports, and they often turn to the things they know, the things they did as kids – swimming, biking, and running. You can swim, bike, or run separately, but when you put these sports together, it adds some adventure. Triathlon makes things a little more interesting. Plus, if you're looking for endurance, or if you're looking for that hard thing, triathlon is it.

But triathlon is also about community, and that is what draws people to it. As we become older adults, we look for our tribe. We look for the people who we want to be around and experience things with, the people who understand what it's like being a parent or being an executive or a professional. Triathlon comes with all types of people, so when you participate in it, you don't just get a sport, you get a family or a community.

The community aspect of triathlon is not always what outsiders see. The sport started with a competitive, elite mentality and image. But today, that makes up a small percentage of who is participating. The age-grouper style of racing is what makes triathlon what it is today.

*So what does the triathlon community look like, really?*

There are pro triathletes – athletes who are paid to do triathlon as their job. They go out there every day, and training is their work. They interact with and inspire athletes and work with brands while being highly competitive within the sport. When they win races, they continue to progress in their career as a professional athlete.

Then there is a small number of elite athletes. These are generally the people with alpha mentalities who take triathlon very seriously. The elites are looking for that edge – the right shoes, the right equipment, the newest technology, the best coach. But they don't do triathlons for a living.

The majority is made up of intermediates and beginners. Those intermediate, middle-of-the-pack athletes enjoy pushing themselves and setting their own personal records and goals, and they're not racing anyone but themselves in most cases.

Then there's the first-timer or the beginner. That first-timer is thinking, "Okay, I'm gonna do my first triathlon. I'm in my first season, and this is who I am. Let's see how this goes."

*I'm a beginner. Can I really do this?*

Henry Ford said, "Whether you think you can, or you think you can't – you're right."

That answers the question. Personally, I said I would never do a full Ironman, but I changed my thinking, and now I'm an Ironman several times over.

**Let's get a few things out of the way:**

1)  If you're scared of triathlon, we can fix that.

Fear is one of the biggest reasons people don't get started with triathlon – or anything else new in life. But remember, you couldn't always run or walk. You had to crawl first. In every stage of life, no matter what it is, we have to learn the process, and we can't be afraid to do things that we've never done because, otherwise, we'll never accomplish anything.

Take swimming, for example. A lot of people are not taught how to swim as children. The reasons could be cultural, or maybe they're opportunity-based. It honestly could be so many things when it comes to swimming, including race and equality and inclusion. (It gets deep really quick when we talk about swimming.) But, just like you've learned to do everything else in life, swimming is the same. Sometimes, you only can't because you haven't tried. So it's not that you can't swim. It's that you can't swim, yet.

Don't let fear guide your decisions. Be curious about what you want to become; be curious about what your body can do; be curious about what your mind can do and what you can tackle when determination is your main objective.

2) Yes, triathlon can be expensive, but it doesn't have to be.

Triathlon can be an expensive sport. There's plenty of interest in the new gear, gadgets, clothing, swag, and toys. There's a very lucrative market in that area, and it's easy to think everyone has all the cool stuff because that's what the marketers want folks to see. They don't show the people doing their first triathlon on a beach cruiser, buying goggles at Walmart, and using the shoes that they have. They don't show those people all the time, but trust me, they exist. Also, not all races cost $800 to enter. There are plenty out there for 50-100 bucks.

It's also a matter of choices. Think about those extras in your day, the fancy coffees, for instance. If you saved your coffee money, you might be able to get a used bike, a new helmet, race and training fuel, running shoes, or a swimsuit. You can probably do a triathlon for under $200. You just have to be creative. It's like everything else in life – just because it's hard, doesn't mean you can't do it. Don't make excuses for why you can't make it happen.

3)  Yes, it's time-consuming. You can find a way.

I always ask: "How much time are you willing to commit to training weekly?"

If someone tells me five hours, I'll ask: "Is that five hours of actual training, or five hours including travel and getting dressed before and/or after?"

Sometimes we overlook those extra pieces that are time zappers, and you have to consider all of that when you make a plan. And then your plan is YOUR plan. When I got started in triathlon, I was trying to do it like everybody else and was hyper-focused on the things I thought I had to do, which were all based on other people's lives. It nearly killed my marriage. Hell, it nearly killed my sanity.

And then I got a coach, and he was like, "Oh, we got to have family first," and that became my motto, as both an athlete and a coach, because without your family and its support, why continue training?

A coach's job is to relieve stress, not put it on you. So I look closely at the time my athletes have. You should do the same thing. Look at your training and look at the time commitment. Ask yourself, *How can I make this efficient?* If you have only 30 minutes a day, you can still do something with that. You might not be able to train for Ironman, but you could train for a sprint or Olympic-distance race. There are so many things that you can make happen, if you choose to make it work.

In this book, we'll delve deeper into these discussions, common hurdles, and questions. You will learn from athletes who are like you and who know the joy that triathlon brings. In each chapter, you'll read real-life, relatable stories, and you'll be given quotes and mantras to consider and use for focus and inspiration. Each chapter also contains a call to action, and many include journal prompts, so you can use this book as a workbook toward your triathlon goals and more.

Triathlon is an adventure that will test your limits and repay you in confidence, pride, friendship, respect, health, and happiness. Get ready. This book is your first step toward the starting line.

# CHAPTER 1
## READY, SET, BE VULNERABLE!

**Core value:** Vulnerability

**Growth quote:** "When you are looking for the answer, look within first."

**Call to action:** Write down one area in your life that you should be more open and vulnerable with yourself about.

**Mantra:** I am the solution.

Two traits are necessary to get a successful start in triathlon: 1) the ability to work within and utilize a team and 2) vulnerability. These two things work together.

The team concept is a huge piece for anybody in the sport, even those who do things solo. Motivation, as well as the sharing of knowledge, technology, and experiences, all come from teammates and the triathlete community, and you have to be willing and open to that. It makes you better because you're not closed off from learning things from other people.

Teams and communities are made up of individuals, though. So for now, let's focus on you, and that starts with vulnerability.

To be successful within the world of triathlon, you need to be vulnerable. You need to be introspective and open up physically, mentally, emotionally, and spiritually. You limit yourself when you are not vulnerable, when you're not able to ask yourself, *What do I need to be better at? And how can I get better at it? Who can help me be better?* Ask those questions and be willing to learn.

Vulnerability is linked to confidence. I've observed many triathletes who come into the sport lacking confidence in areas of their lives, so they use triathlons to build confidence that they can transfer to their personal relationships, their families, their professions, or other athletic things.

Confidence is the completion of hard things. And that's what competency is, too. The higher mountains you climb, the more confident you become. When you look at triathlon, it's more complex, more strategic, and more thought-provoking than doing a solo run, ride, or swim. When you complete these things together, you think, *I am stronger than I thought I was. I am capable.*

But doubt can remain. You'll see people around you succeeding, but you can't help wondering, *They are doing it, but can I?*

You may think you should push away that doubt, or overcome it somehow. But doubt can be a good thing.

There's a healthy amount of doubt that exists in all of us. But if you sit in doubt, that is totally different. If you sit in despair, that is totally different. If you sit in grief, that is totally different. If you sit in depression, that is totally different. The key is to recognize that these things exist and do what it takes to move through them.

I don't know an athlete on this planet who has done anything – from the smallest to the biggest thing – who wasn't trying to challenge the status quo, themselves, or the standard. There's a level of doubt that calls the question: *Can I be the one to do this?*

The key is, don't let this question overwhelm you. Don't let self-doubt or low self-confidence leave you stagnant. Allow it to ignite the flame, so you can accomplish anything.

In my experience, women embrace vulnerability more easily than men do. I talk to thousands of people. When I talk to men, they don't want to get deep into things like vulnerability and self-confidence. They might agree at the moment, but then they run from the truth. I get it. As a man, especially as a Marine, I didn't like getting vulnerable, either, in the beginning. It felt like weakness, and in my world, weakness can get you killed.

Vulnerability to a man is often lonely, scary, and overwhelming. But on the other side, it's freeing. It's like a thousand smiles. It is joy unleashed. When you've bottled up your emotions and perceived weaknesses for your whole life, once you let them out, you finally get to be yourself and know yourself.

Because inside, we're all thinking the same things. We have the same doubts. No matter what anyone's gender

*Barbara Ogle*

is, we want the same thing – to be better. Women just seem more willing to accept that and live that truth.

I work with a woman named Barbara, who, when she first came to me, blamed everyone else for her shortcomings. It was always someone else's fault why she couldn't do things, or why she didn't have time, or why she wasn't successful. "The problem isn't them," I told her. "The problem is you!"

She wasn't a bad person, of course. But the more we talked, the more it was apparent that she was living her life for others, especially her loved ones. I helped her understand that she didn't have to live like that. "The only person you need to live for is yourself," I told her, "and the people who love you will accept you for who you are."

As Barbara took responsibility for herself, she started to feel better about herself. She started to realize, *It's not the other people. I'm allowing them to make me feel the way I'm feeling, and I don't have to do that. I should start taking responsibility for my own health, instead of taking care of other people, and then having no one to take care of me.*

Most people are not willing to say, "I'm the problem." What realization could be more vulnerable? But if you can admit that, and if you can accept that you have a part to play in your own life, then you write your own story. Otherwise, you will always be living with other people's expectations, and whatever they write for you, and that's not what was meant to be.

Barbara agrees. "Frustration comes when you don't have time for yourself," she explains. "You don't have the energy because you've given it all away."

That first step, being open and vulnerable like Barbara, is a big one. But the first physical steps don't have to be huge. Barbara signed up for a race, and to get ready, she started with small things – adding meditation into her day, walking 3,000 steps. We built these things into her schedule.

For everyone, those first practical steps toward a successful triathlon will look different, but they can look like these most foundational things.

When we first started working together, Barbara was stretched thin with responsibilities at work, volunteering, her family, and church. I told her, "Pick four things. No one can do more than four things well, and right now, you have, like, 30."

"I had to figure out what was truly essential," Barbara says. "I asked myself, *If I don't do this, is anyone actually going to die?* And the answer was always, *No.* I didn't have to be the lifesaver on every project."

Realizing this allowed Barbara to prioritize herself, and, it turns out, it was her own life that she likely saved.

During the early months of the Covid-19 pandemic, Barbara stayed on track – that is, until she didn't. "I was steady from January to September," she remembers. "And then, all of a sudden, like a lot of people who were burned out and exhausted by everything going on in the world, I was just done."

She gave herself the mental break she felt she needed, and she stopped training. And then, like a lot of people, she got Covid.

"I was, like, *Oh, crap!*" Barbara says. "*I have Type 2 diabetes. I'm obese. I have all these things. I should be dead.*"

There was hopeful news, though. As part of her treatment, doctors looked at her heart, and "my heart was freaking amazing," she says. Her heart was in good shape as a direct result of doing triathlon, and it's what likely saved her life, the doctors told her.

But then what?

Deconditioned from Covid and the long layoff from training posed a daunting reality for Barbara. For a while, just the walk from her bedroom to her kitchen left her out of breath. It was discouraging and frightening and made her feel more vulnerable than ever. As much as it hurt to admit it, she was starting over.

"Look, you're not going to be running marathons right now," I told her. And then we broke down her training to the basics again, with a gradual buildup. It's not easy to start over, so we came up with a few tricks to help shape Barbara's perspective.

For instance, it helped to count steps in a day instead of recording distance.

"If I had to do two miles, that seemed like a lot," Barbara recalls. "But if I had to do 6,000 steps, that felt more doable, even when 6,000 steps is farther than two miles."

Little things like that are what helped Barbara get back on track and recover from her time away from triathlon. Sometimes you just need to start over, but rarely will you be starting again from square one, even after serious illness or injury. None of the time you put in will be wasted.

Restarts always account for the learning and work you've invested, so if you're lucky, you can jump into your learning curve at a point closer to your goal. And remember, even if you start over 1,000 times, you at least went somewhere.

Barbara is building back to where she once was, and she's mentoring other women in the sport. She's a living example of how being vulnerable and open in every sense of the word brings value to the triathlon community and each individual athlete.

# CHAPTER 2
## FINDING YOUR WHY → MOTIVATION

**Core values:** Vulnerability, enthusiasm

**Growth quote:** "When you know why you are, you will know who you are."

**Call to action:** Write down why you do what you do, how you do it, and what/who you do it for.

**Mantra:** Open my heart, find my purpose.

The way I teach people is by asking questions. And then I listen. Really listen.

I ask them, "What is your *why* in life?" Because from the *why* comes the *how* and the *what*.

A lot of people focus on the *what*, which is the end goal. How many times have you asked yourself, *What do I want to do? What do I want to have?* Probably a lot. But have you asked yourself how you're going to reach that end goal, or why you want it in the first place?

When you answer your *why*, you will have found your purpose. An easy and obvious answer I often hear

*Ryan Anderson*

when I ask someone what their *why* is, "I want to set an example for my kids."

"But why do you want to set an example?" I'll challenge.

They almost always say that they've experienced something that caused suffering in a way they don't want their children to know. And that if the kids do something like a triathlon (after seeing Mom or Dad do it), they might not ever experience the same pain or conflict.

They say this because they understand the intrinsics of triathlon. Deep down, they want their children to experience the satisfaction, the joy, the sense of accomplishment, the pride ... all the good feelings that come from completing a task or goal or hard thing, and in doing so, perhaps the kids will repeat positive and correct choices that'll keep them from the dark places their parents know.

That's a whole lot more powerful than just wanting to set an example by swimming, biking, and running.

The physical component of triathlon is what people see. But it's the mental and emotional pieces that are key to having an amazing athlete journey. That's why finding your *why* is so important. Because once you know your *why*, you'll tap into your true motivation.

I work with an athlete named Ryan. He's a Marine, and he was a runner as a kid. As an adult, though, he got blown up in Iraq, and he walked with a cane for a while after that. When I met him, he was trying to get fit, but he was overweight, introverted, and never really smiled. He didn't really believe in himself.

The first time we worked out together, I remember him saying, "I don't know if I can do this."

"You don't know until you try," I told him, and I knew we had to find his *why*.

Ryan has children, so the obvious and first *why* was his kids. I went with it.

"You don't want them to see you give up," I told him, and he finished that first workout.

But, like many people, Ryan had a deeper *why* – his health.

"You have been given a second chance, man," I told him. "What are you going to do with that?"

Getting to the bottom of that question is what gave him his spark, his motivation. And in this case, at least in the beginning, the answer was defiance.

Ryan was determined to show the doctors wrong, and in the process, prove to himself that he would get back to what he considered and remembered to be normal. He already was walking unassisted, which no one thought he'd do again, but he was running too, and soon he was biking and swimming.

As Ryan's accomplishments stacked up, his own self-worth and self-appreciation grew. Ryan always had the love and support of his family, but he had struggled to love himself. Now that he proved to himself and others what he can do, I see him smile.

Ryan's *why* has evolved and grown from his earliest days in triathlon. Today, he's a coach as well as an athlete, and he finds motivation in helping other people change and better their lives like he did. One of those people is his youngest son, who has cerebral palsy.

"Where I'm at now," Ryan says, "really shows him that no matter what somebody says, you're only defined by what you limit yourself to be. I work as hard as I do and have become a coach because I want to help myself, my son, and others get to a point where they can be comfortable in their skin."

Your *why* doesn't have to be like Ryan's. No matter what yours is, though, it's important to know that motivation is temporary. Motivation is only the urge to start. I often hear, "I had the motivation, but now it's gone."

Motivation requires immediate action – forward movement.

So when you have an idea, you can't just sit on it. Say a race catches your attention. You think, *I'm going to get in shape and do that.* But you have to do more than think. Take action. Sign up for the race! Call someone and tell them. Post about it on social media. Buy the shoes. Make an appointment with your coach. You're motivated, right? That spark isn't going to last forever. You have to act, because how many times have you done all those steps and failed to keep it moving? Here's the thing about motivation: You have to feed it. You have to shift into a bigger gear.

Ryan has done that quite literally. His exposure to triathlon led to an interest in nutrition, and now he's in school to become a dietitian. The more he studies, the more he can offer as a coach, and that feeds the motivation loop for him.

"Being able to help others reclaim their lives really is my goal," he says.

There's another piece to the motivation puzzle: consistency. You have to keep going.

One way to achieve consistency is to add accountability to the picture. We'll talk more about teamwork and tribes in a later chapter, but here's a sneak peek: The first step is to surround yourself and train with people who will say, "You can do this," and "Let's go!" This type of encouragement feeds motivation and helps reestablish your *why*. Before long, as you keep showing up for the people who show up for you, motivation turns into dedication, and that's where the magic happens.

# CHAPTER 3
## DEDICATION AND HARMONY

**Core values**: Perseverance, enthusiasm

**Growth quote**: "Don't seek to find balance; seek to embrace harmony."

**Call to action:** Email Coach Morgon and explain how you create harmony in your life. (info@morgonlatimore.com)

**Mantra:** Harmony is freedom.

People often throw words around without really thinking about what they mean. Let's take the word *balance*, for instance.

Balance comes up in a lot of conversations with triathletes. "I gotta find some balance with this and the other things in my life," is what I'll hear a lot.

It's easy to get wrapped up in the triathlete lifestyle. Trust me, once you start feeling stronger, all you want is more of that feeling. Plus, triathlon, by nature of being hard and challenging, attracts people who tend to go all in, and being committed can come at the expense of other responsibilities and the people in your life.

*Morgon Latimore*

So balance, right? Wrong. Balance has a tipping point. When you have two sides competing for dominance, everybody's going to lose sometime, and that's stressful. So ditch the balancing act. Instead of balance, aim for harmony.

I like the word *harmony*. It means that things work together instead of taking turns. When things are in harmony, they are fluid, so that is easier. When things feel easier, that's when you get longevity – in anything, really – but in this case, in your athletic career.

Achieving harmony is all about prioritizing and getting creative. I've already mentioned how I used to go overboard with my training and racing, putting personal relationships in jeopardy. I thought there'd always be a chance after practice, after racing, to make up for the time lost. But the reality was that I wasn't finding a way to balance sport and the people who were important to me. Sport was winning, and family was losing.

I remember finishing one of my first races and not even looking at or thanking or acknowledging my family, who had picked up the slack for me for months and who were still cheering for me at the finish line. I didn't even hug them. It was not my finest moment, and I regret it, except for how much it taught me.

After being called out, I recognized that I was not being the kind of athlete – the kind of *person* – I wanted to be, and that I not only was confusing balance and harmony, but also commitment with dedication.

You'll hear coaches tell athletes all the time, "You

gotta be committed, and then you'll see the results." It makes sense, and sure, there's some truth to it. You have to practice to get better. But what is commitment?

It's an obligation.

When I first started triathlon, I felt obligated to train as much as I could and stay laser-focused on my goals, thinking that was the way to prove my commitment to the sport, which I believed was the way to be most successful.

But to whom did I have to prove things? And who likes having more obligations on their plate? No one and nobody. My commitment was making me a miserable person to be around, and that needed to change.

I wasn't willing to just give it up, though. *I'm stronger, healthier and smarter since starting this sport,* I thought to myself. *But why would I dedicate so much time and effort and study, just to have it result in unhappiness?*

The answer to that question goes to the heart of what dedication really is. It's devotion. And devotion is love. I loved my sport, and I loved my family, so I needed to get those things working together – to put them in harmony.

I reigned things in, started putting family first. And then, when I began training for my next race, my outlook and goals were different. I asked myself, *How can I do both?* I had to get creative, so I invited my family with me. My daughters and my wife now sometimes go on bike rides with me. My daughters go to my races and help on the course. I always acknowledge their interest and support, and I never forget to say, "thank you."

No, they don't always tag along, and that's fine. I do my longest workouts when they are busy with other things, so we're all getting what we need and want. I'm working out more often and more efficiently now than when I thought commitment required all-in at the expense of all else.

I'm always working on achieving harmony, but the mind shift to dedication over commitment was a game-changer. I'm lucky for the chance to have grown from my experience, and maybe that's the moral to this story: Don't count on being lucky. Don't fall into the intensity trap that I did. The goal is longevity, the outcome of triathlon's core value of perseverance, and longevity is not sustainable without dedication and harmony.

A couple of other thoughts about perseverance:

By definition, *perseverance* is doing something despite it being difficult or there being a delay in achieving success. Therefore, perseverance is patience. It's knowing that if you keep showing up (being dedicated) and pushing through, success awaits.

With perseverance as your backbone, is anything in life truly hard or unachievable? No. For if you persevere, you can get through anything, and on the other side will be success and celebration.

Ok, but how, exactly, do you persevere when your workouts or races don't go well?

I've worked with a lot of athletes who believe that their situation is so distraught, so unique, that no one could ever understand, and no one else has ever gone through anything similar. A lot of athletes think that when things get difficult, it means they're not supposed to be there.

I have to remind them – and myself sometimes – that each time you push through the hard stuff – an injury, a scheduling setback, an emotional tidal wave – you add a layer of resilience that you can call on and peel back like an onion to reveal renewed strength when you need it. So at the root of perseverance is reflection.

It's important when you're remembering all you've achieved to keep focused on the positive. It's easy to think about the hard times, and to let your mind sink into thoughts of *Oh, man, that was the worst time ever.* But what good does that kind of thinking do?

Each achievement in your athletic journey is something you can look back on to help propel you forward. Connect with your past challenges to create your own longevity in the sport. When you patiently and positively persevere, anything is possible.

# CHAPTER 4
## ARE WE HAVING FUN, YET?

**Core values:** Adventure, enthusiasm

---

**Growth quote:** "If you are not enjoying what you do, why do it at all?"

---

**Call to action:** Once a week do one thing that you consider fun other than swimming, biking, or running.

---

**Mantra:** Have fun!

The Marine Corps defines *enthusiasm* as "a display of sincere interest or exuberance in the performance of what you do." It's one of the Corps' leadership principles and traits, and what it boils down to is that enthusiasm is celebration. Enthusiasm is celebrating growth, celebrating learning, even celebrating failures, depending on how you look at them.

I carry the same definition into triathlon. So you'll see me talking to everyone, learning their stories, high-fiving people at the finish line. I want people to notice my exuberance, too. You'll see me always in bright tri kits and flashy socks, and always with a loud voice full of congratulations and affirmations.

Everyone wants to hear someone telling them, "Great job!" And I think we, as athletes, triathletes, and coaches, need to say and hear that every day. We need to not only be enthusiastic and share that enthusiasm, but we need to live it – be happy that we get to move.

I tell people, "Be happy that you woke up. Be happy that you can breathe. You might not be able to run as fast as you think you should, but that's not what you should be focused on. You should be happy that you have the ability to complain."

*Enthusiasm* is the word to remind us that we should be celebrating every part of our journey, that we should be engaged in the positive side because the world gives us enough of the negative. Some people will never get the chance to do a triathlon.

I know it's not always sunshine and cotton candy. Sometimes, you can get sucked up in disappointment, agony, or dread. Enthusiasm can be hard to come by.

You might think, *Well, I suck at this.*

I'll be honest. I've been there. Remember that race when I didn't hug my family at the end? There was a lot going on in my life then. I'd just come back from being deployed in Afghanistan. I was coaching a little on top of being an athlete, but I still felt alone and angry, especially at people who didn't appreciate their health or wellness.

When I heard triathletes complain or blame their

poor performance on something like not having the right shoes, my response would be like, "At least you got feet."

I approached triathlon with a Marine-like, task-oriented mentality – just get the job done – and as much as I loved it for what it did for my body and mind, it was joyless. I was joyless. I didn't yet understand what I was a part of, or what I was doing.

A mentor of mine saw I was struggling and talked to me about the impact we all have on others.

"Someone is always watching," he said. "And you, by your actions, can change their life."

I knew his words were true. I was a leader in the Marine Corps, and I knew that if I wanted to see change in someone, I had to set the example. I had to be the change I wanted to see.

As I developed that train of thought, I learned that the more enthusiastic I acted about training and racing, the more I enjoyed it. The more I enjoyed it, the more value it brought to me and the people around me. Over time, triathlon became less about competition and more about the smile I'd see on someone's face.

Then, I became intentional about creating excitement, and I noticed that the enthusiasm that I'd show was the energy people would replicate. I became the high-fiving, loud athlete/coach who would dance and celebrate the people around me, and guess what? People would do that for me, too. And it makes the whole thing FUN.

*Akila O'Grady*

I had a coach once say, "I'm not here to be a cheerleader."

To that, I say, "So what are you here for, then?"

I truly believe that endurance sports, triathlons, even swimming, are just our way, as adults, to get that ribbon like we got in third grade. We're just trying to re-create those happy moments and feelings. And it's great to have someone cheering for you, whether you win or lose.

What is it about earning a ribbon for a race as a child? Part of what makes that slip of shiny fabric special is that it acknowledges success in an adventure, something that maybe you've never done before, but tried, anyway.

Triathlon is the grown-up version of that. Each race poses a new adventure, for sure, but so does every interaction within the event. You can break each race into slivers of time – in the swim corral, at the transitions, or on the run, for instance. It's in these passing segments that you interact and have adventures with people. Maybe someone tells you they're nervous before the swim, or they need help in the transition area. You'll problem-solve and encourage and support, and those actions are adventures. Sharing adventures is how you make friends in triathlon.

I work with an athlete named Akila who is the epitome of adventure and enthusiasm in triathlon. She pushes me as a coach because she's always looking for the hardest, craziest races and challenges. (Like, she wanted to run 40 miles on her 40th birthday. She clued me into this plan three weeks before.)

Akila likes to find races that support charity. This is her *why*, and it gets her motivated. Putting in the work for others also boosts her enthusiasm for her efforts.

"I always say to people, 'I never run for free,' Akila says. "I'm never going to wake up and do 140.6 miles just because it's fun. The reality of the matter is, I'm just not that girl."

It's not about the podium, she added. "It's about the journey and about pulling people along with me, and also giving back."

Akila raises both funds and awareness on her athlete journey, specifically in memory of a young nephew and cousin who both died. She wears their names and the names of other children on her racing kit because they are dear to her heart. That way, she says, she recognizes that while her race might be hard, "other parents and other children might have it way harder than I do."

She also uses her events to raise money for autism causes.

"For me," she explains, "it makes the whole thing more enjoyable because I'm not out there running for free or out there running just for fun. I'm doing it for something bigger than me."

Akila's friends and training partners know how she likes to go big, so when she announced her 40-for-40th plan, they worked to make it fun for her. Two ran it with her and rallied behind the scenes to have friends planted along the route – a big birthday surprise for the woman who goes big for everyone else.

"There were all these people," Akila recalled. "It was amazing."

It was also a prime example of what Akila says is key to making and keeping triathlon enjoyable: having a support system. "I do all this crazy stuff," she says, "but I can't do it without the people around me."

# CHAPTER 5
## TEAMWORK AND TRIBES

**Core values:** Community, encouragement

**Growth quote**: "We are a team when we bring value to each other."

**Call to action:** Tell those on your team that you appreciate and value them. Make this a habit.

**Mantra:** We are stronger together.

I'm always trying to be independent, but it never really feels good. I didn't realize until I was in my late 30s that even though I'm a self-starter and very motivated, those qualities don't make me happy. I found out late that I really like having partnerships, and knowing that makes me think of my dad, who always said, "Two heads are better than one."

When I put this into practice with triathlon, it adds value to my experience. Sure, anyone can swim, bike, or run on their own, but when you do it with the right people, it creates a more in-depth experience full of wisdom and knowledge and culture. I like to think of this as "finding your tribe."

Your tribe can be made up of people you know, but some of the most valuable ones expose you to foreign ideas and ways of thinking. Consider this: Triathlon is unique in that it has international reach and opportunity for the average athlete. Unlike other adult sports, where to travel and meet people far from home, you have to earn a spot or advance through championship ranks, triathlon is open and available to everyone.

I work with athletes from around the world, in places as varied as Argentina, Japan, and Colombia. Triathlon connects us, and I have learned so much about myself by getting to know these people. Triathlon, for me, has been a melting pot of awesomeness.

At races, I see all types of people working toward the same goals. It blows my mind, and my heart bursts with happiness to see all types of people all at the same event, all doing their best and supporting each other. As the world is changing and waking up to issues of race and inclusion these days, triathlon is proving to be a good representative of that diversity.

How do you find your tribe within the triathlon melting pot? Research. The obvious place is to look for triathlon groups on the internet or social media, but don't forget to look for individual-sport groups, too. I guarantee you that cycling clubs and swim clubs and run clubs all have triathletes in them. There's a lot of cross-pollination.

When you find a group that interests you, plan to spend 30 or 60 days getting to know them. Train with them; go to lunch; see how they interact. This is not the time to commit to them, though. Plan to test out up to three groups over a few months. Be picky. You're looking for your triathlon family.

Evaluate each group for the logistical stuff – where and when they meet and what types of events they do (sprint, Olympic, Ironman) – and also the extras like social gatherings and whether the club gives back to the community, both the local community and the overall endurance-sport community. Observe and listen for any drama within the group, and if there's anything you don't feel good about, that's a red flag. Be careful to only interject yourself in the parts of the organization that are important to you and enhance your experience.

One thing that intimidates a lot of new people is how much a group is focused on performance. Take a good look at the skill levels of the athletes in any group that you are considering, and make sure there's a place for you. I hear about training groups that will be encouraging to new people, but in reality, they might leave you in the dust. If that happens, that's not the group for you. You need to find the people who are at the same skill level, or at least are willing to help you improve and move up.

Once you find the group you like, this is your chance to learn and lean into the sport. Group training helps keep you accountable and motivated, and you'll have a built-in cheering section on top of, usually, access to coaching advice. Don't hesitate to ask questions – most of what you learn will add value to your journey.

*Patricia Howe*

Some people might think social media groups can provide the same kind of information sharing, but I'd caution you about that. If you go into a triathlon social media group and ask a question, maybe about the right kind of shoes to wear, you might get 4,000 answers to that question. It's too much.

Don't let a group of strangers overwhelm you with advice. Find your trusted tribe and keep your circle of advisors small. No one has time for the chaos of unknown social media "experts."

I work with an athlete named Patricia, who describes herself as "not a member of clubs." She remembers going with a couple of friends to a triathlon club meeting and being overwhelmed by tutus, chanting and cheering, and sad stories.

"This is not the group for me," she thought at the time.

The group, it turns out, was dedicated to helping women complete their first triathlon. They focused on mentoring, and Patricia and her friends had shown up for the first meeting of the training season.

Her instinct was to run away, but she didn't. This was already her second go-round with triathlon. For the first, she had signed up for an event, recruited some friends, and then never trained and didn't compete. On race day, her friends finished, but Patricia watched from the sideline. She'd been kicking herself since.

So, despite the soulful testimonials and crazy costumes, she stuck with it, and two things happened: 1) She had her two friends to be her immediate and familiar support crew and training partners, and 2) she saw just how supportive and uplifting the larger group was, and it made her want to be a part of it.

"When I would go to running events or swimming events, there were people from this group there, and they cared about me and asked about me," she said. "And if I wanted to go swim somewhere, there would be people already going, so I didn't have to be afraid of showing up somewhere new.

"This group of folks wanted us to succeed, and they were cheering for us the whole time."

As she kept showing up, Patricia found herself being overwhelmed again – this time in a good way – by the group's kindness. She found herself wanting to give back, too. "I started to think about others more than I thought about myself," she says. "I got hooked on the idea of helping others do triathlons."

Today, Patricia makes a point to notice the first-timers and others who hang back or stand alone, who maybe look put off or unimpressed by the boisterous nature of the club. She sees herself in them, and she knows if they bolt, they will miss out. She has advice for anyone feeling that way:

"Please, walk up to somebody," she insists. "Don't judge a book by its cover.

"I wasn't comfortable with the (boisterous nature of the) group, and then I realized that wasn't what defined the group – that really wasn't what it was all about. It certainly did make me want to run for the hills because, yeah, I wasn't feeling it at first. I laugh about that today.

"The wrapping on it might not always be your thing, but it's worth it to get past that," she assures.

The right tribe makes you realize you're not doing this alone. One of the best things about that, Patricia claims, is that when she's having a down day, she can put her thoughts on someone else, and not worry about herself.

"It's crazy how much more I can do," she says, "because I'm thinking about pulling somebody along on a bike, or I'm thinking about running a pace. It really is the true definition of the team."

Patricia is grateful she didn't quit after that first day for reasons beyond her athletic achievements. To her, it's about health and the bonus that comes from giving back to the team she now considers her tribe.

"I've been able to participate in life events for people, good and bad, and support them through them, things which I may not have been willing to cross over and get involved in before. It has really opened my eyes to how much this community needs you beyond the advice about your swim stroke."

# CHAPTER 6
## YOU ARE ENOUGH → SELF-BELIEF

**Core values**: Value, peace

---

**Growth quote**: To have great success, you must believe that it's possible for you.

---

**Call to action**:  Every night, 15 minutes before going to bed, write, "I am enough" in a notebook. Keep the notebook on the side of your bed. Do this for 29 days.

Consider these journaling prompts: Why is being enough important? Have you ever felt like you weren't enough? What did you do to change that belief? What steps can athletes take to start feeling like they are enough?

---

**Mantra:** I am enough.

A lot of people don't get into triathlon because they don't think they have what it takes. In this chapter, I'm going to take down this way of thinking, and like a lot of things in this book, the ideas I'm going to address seep outside of the athletic realm.

When you don't think you're enough in one thing (like triathlon), it's very likely that you don't think you're enough in a lot of other places in your life, too. You might second-guess if you have what it takes to be a good mother, to be a good father, to be a good athlete, to be a good employee, to be a good boss. You might be on a journey to find out what you are, who you are, and what you are capable of doing, yet self-doubt like this can keep you from even trying or getting started in the first place.

The questions you have often come from the outside. Parents, family, friends ... everyone cares about what the important people in their life think of them. But sadly, these thoughts are often judgemental and negative and help to shape the way you think about yourself.

I've seen it a lot. When the people around you have stuff in their own lives that keeps them from thinking things are possible, that will spill over into your life, too. Many people think they can't be a runner or a swimmer or a cyclist because the environment around them dictates what they are capable of. When the people around them show a lack of support in their actions and words, that creates low self-confidence and a lack of self-belief.

But just because your environment might be like that, it doesn't mean it has to be that way forever. Let's take swimming as an example. There are whole communities of people who don't swim, and who don't believe they *can* swim, especially among people of color in the United States. There are lots of reasons for this, but it is often perpetuated because of unintentional or unconscious bias, even from within the non-swimming community itself. There's a belief that because it's "always been this way," it's OK to continue that way. This type of thinking gives energy to stereotypes and makes life stagnant.

I've been challenged in my work as a Marine to take on biases like these, and the same tenets I use in my professional life can be applied to triathlon. If you find yourself thinking you are not capable of doing triathlon because people like you typically don't do the sport, there's a three-part strategy to overcoming those thoughts: detect, reflect and reject.

Let's look at that more closely.

**Detect the stereotype**. Recognize it, and if it's you doing the stereotyping, own it. Don't believe you can swim because no one in your family swims? That's pretty common. And maybe those family members are giving you a hard time for aspiring to do it, too. Also common. But none of that has to make it true.

Instead of buying into the negativity, **reflect on the stereotype**. Where does it come from? Realize that it's hard to not project fears and beliefs about yourself onto others, and it's equally hard to see success in others when you don't see it for or in yourself. That's what is often going on when your family and friends don't support your goals.

While your environment and upbringing make you who you are, you can change your environment and be somebody different. You can **reject the stereotypes** and expectations of and for your community. It's hard to change as an adult – you might have years of negative thoughts and beliefs etched in your head. But at the most basic of levels in this example, sign up for a swim lesson. And then show up. That is how you move forward.

Here's the truth: We decide our own fate. We decide our own destiny by the choices that we make, and believing that you are enough is more about self-fulfillment than it is about proving someone else wrong. Believing in yourself is worth it, no matter what anyone else thinks.

I practice this in my personal life, too. After more than two decades in the Marine Corps, I am transitioning to retirement, and I'm scared. The civilian world is foreign to me – just like the starting line of a triathlon once was.

I feel inadequate in a lot of ways. My anxiety is high. People tell me I'll be fine outside the Corps, but that's hard to believe.

A colleague told me recently, "You're only focusing on all the things that could go wrong. How about you start to focus on all the things you've done right to get yourself to this point?"

She was telling me to reflect on my truths and to reject the worst-case scenarios. She knows I've done the work to have a successful post-military life. Now it's time for me to believe it, too.

So I tell myself every day, *I've done enough. I am enough.* And I say it out loud to whoever will listen. I speak it into existence. I truly believe that whatever you want to occur in life, you have to live it, you have to breathe it, you have to bleed it.

At the root of this is preparation. If you are prepared — if you've done the work — you will start believing that you are capable and that your outcome will be acceptable and successful. This is true at the start of every race or lifetime endeavor. In triathlon, that means doing the training, both physical and mental.

I have struggled with this because fear is real, and it's not always rational. It's not OK to sit in fear, though. On the other side of fear is celebration and accomplishment. On the other side of fear is peace. So I want you to believe me when I tell you, "You are enough." But even more, I want you to believe in yourself when you think, *I am enough.*

I work with an athlete named Angie, and when we first met, she was afraid of the water. She could swim, but she wouldn't go in the deep end of the pool. She'd learned to swim only in the few months before I met her, and before that, she'd been scared to even get her face wet in the shower.

So, obviously, she'd already come a long way in her swimming journey, but every time she tried to swim the length of the pool, she would stop where she could see the bottom drop off.

On the first day we worked together, I put two chairs at the side of the pool, right where there was a line dividing the shallow from the deep. We sat and talked about how Black people don't think they can swim or even *should* swim. We reflected on how, in reality, West

*Angie Jackson*

Africans were some of the greatest watermen in history, and how it's our African American culture that has developed fear for the deep side of the line.

I told her, "We can choose to not develop fear, too."

When we got in the water, she froze up a little bit. "I don't know what the problem is," she said.

"As soon as you choose to believe in yourself," I told her, "you will cross that line." And I backed away from her.

"Where are you going?" she asked.

"You need your space," I told her. "When you make the choice, I'll be here."

Angie came into that swim lesson ready to make a change in her life, and when she swam over that line to the deep end, it was transformative. She knew at that moment that she was enough, no matter what anyone else said or expected of her.

"I had the ability to go farther," Angie recalls. "I just didn't believe in myself. Until that day, I wanted to stay comfortable where I was, but once I realized I had a choice, I was, like, 'I don't choose to stay back here.'"

Angie remembers another self-belief breakthrough, this one at a murky lake where she usually trains with her triathlete team. One day, she found herself there by herself, wetsuit on and swim buoy in hand, and she told herself, "I'm just going to do it. I'm going to swim around."

Around would be a mile, and to date, she'd only swum

across, a much shorter distance.

She got started, swimming through cold spots that took her breath away and made her panic. She knew the colder water meant the lake was deeper in those areas. *I know I can swim in this*, she reminded herself. *It doesn't matter if it's six feet or 30 feet deep. I'm not going down there, anyway.*

Before long, Angie reached a pier about 600 yards away. She did the math. "If I turned back, I'd be at 1200 yards, which seemed too close to being a mile to not just keep going around," she recalls.

What made Angie believe she could swim the lake's circumference that day? Three things: She trusted her training, believed in herself, and at the same time, she had no expectations.

Only a month prior, Angie had never swum more than 100 yards straight. But over the course of several weeks, she practiced, and she proved to herself she could do more. She kept any pressure to perform at bay, though. So that day at the lake, she had a nonchalant, let's-see-what-happens approach backed up by a solid month of getting better every day.

In other words, she'd put in the work, and she made a choice to keep going.

Her advice to anyone who finds themselves standing on the shore, unsure of the first step toward their goals?

"Don't give up on yourself, and don't stop showing up."

# CHAPTER 7
## CONFRONTING YOUR FEARS

**Core value**: Encouragement

---

**Growth quote**: "Refusing to face your fears is refusing to grow."

---

**Call to action:** When you are afraid, do what you fear, and write down 3-5 positive results.

---

**Mantra:** Move forward.

It's almost cliche to think the scariest part of a triathlon is the swim. Water is so foreign to so many of us that being afraid of the swim is automatic.

But if I were to ask my athletes about their true fears, I doubt swimming would even make the list. Instead, I would hear about more big-picture concerns like fear of failure, fear of not being accepted, fears over body image, fear of being too old, and even fear of outright death.

That's a lot to worry about, and all of it is valid. At the same time, it's not OK to sit in fear and let it rule your decisions. Confronting and dealing with your fears will allow you to be the best triathlete you can be, and once fears are at bay, you will be surprised how other aspects of your life open up and improve, too.

Let's take a deeper look at each of the common fears listed above.

### What if I blow it?

Some people think failure will define them. Like, if they fail once, they are going to continue to fail. This is a very daunting feeling. It's like a great cloud that hovers. If this is how you think, no matter how much you train, you never feel that success is possible.

It's overwhelming, and in a lot of cases, you can only focus on the things you have done incorrectly. You almost lack the ability to remember the things you have accomplished. It's as if you have shades on that make it hard to see the things that you have achieved that were hard and great.

In triathlon, failure often and obviously takes one of two forms: "Did Not Start" or "Did Not Finish." Both are emotionally tough to reckon with. DNS is easier to accept, though.

Things like injuries, financial commitments, or an inability to travel can keep someone from the starting line, even after the training investment. If an athlete has a pattern of signing up for a race, of making excuses and then not showing up, that's a clue of something bigger going on.

But a DNF tends to be bigger from the get-go.

DNF means a "Did Not Finish" on the results sheet. I've seen DNFs put athletes into deep depression. It can actually make athletes question their capability to live life because they've spent so much time training that they identify themselves firstly as triathletes, and it hurts to not get the success they're looking for.

One of the reasons people do triathlon is because once they do, they feel better about other things in their lives. But I've seen a DNF disrupt that transcendence.

Anything can cause a DNF. Didn't complete the swim? Happens all the time. Or maybe there were mechanical problems on the bike or weather issues on the run. But then the questions come: *Did I not do enough? Am I enough? Should I even be here? Why am I doing this?* You start to believe the naysayers and accept all the negative things that have come with the process instead of fighting through.

*How do I explain this to my kids? How do I tell my wife? How am I going to deal with the people who say, "I told you so"? How am I gonna post it on social media?*

It's hard to reason with why you didn't make it to the end of the race. It's even harder to sit back and watch other people finish what you couldn't. *I was not good enough to be here with these athletes. They're better than me*, you might think.

Getting a DNF is like dying inside. That sounds dramatic, but stay with me. Once a person wraps up their self-identity in their sport, if they do not achieve their goals, who are they then? There's true mourning that goes on, and I've seen DNF triathletes grieve. They won't talk about the DNF, and the people around them don't know what to say. Condolences like, "You'll do better next time," come off as condescending and empty.

So, yeah, fear of failure is legitimate, and it has to be handled delicately. I've seen athletes DNF, and they literally do not come back to the sport for years.

The best way to avoid a DNF is preparation. Planning is important. Discipline is important. Consistency is important. If you've done everything possible in your world that you know to do, then there's nothing to worry about. And then be honest with yourself. A lot of heartbreak over failure can be avoided by being truly honest about your preparation and capabilities. If you're not ready for that Ironman, scale it back to a more appropriate distance.

I remember seeing one guy at my pool years ago, before I started coaching. He couldn't even swim 25 yards without flipping on his back and doing some crazy stroke. But he was training for a full Ironman. On his race day, he didn't make the cutoff for the swim, and he was pulled from the water. He was so mad at himself, but, really, what did he expect?

So be real. You'll save yourself a lot of anger, worry, and fear.

What if you fail anyway? At that point, it's important to learn from the failure and reframe the experience to opportunity. A DNF doesn't have to be a failure. It can be a chance to grow into a better athlete, and there's no reason to be scared of that.

**But I really don't belong here.**

When someone has a fear of not fitting into a triathlon group, I want to say, "Don't worry about what people think of you. People that love you will love you for who you are."

But it's more complicated than that. As much as I want that to be true, and as much as I want saying that to be helpful, you never really know another person's life experiences. You don't know if they've been abused emotionally or physically in childhood or by their spouses or peers. What if they never really fit in at home? Why would they think they would fit in with a bunch of strangers doing swim-bike-run?

So, again, the fear is often logical, and in triathlon, it often reveals itself with internal thoughts of *Am I worthy enough to be in this group?* The question comes up especially when an athlete thinks about joining a group that is faster than they are.

*I can't run with this group*, they might think.

But that doesn't make any sense. If you want to be better, you have to do harder things like joining a more advanced group as you improve. You have to come outside your box, right? I've had to do this myself.

When I competed in the World Ironman 70.3 Championship, even though I earned the right to be alongside the rest of the athletes, I found myself overwhelmed in their presence. This race was for the best in the world, and truth be told, I'm not that fast. *Do I belong here?* I asked myself. *Do I fit in?*

My coach prepared me. "They're going to run past you," he said. "And not just a few of them. Hundreds of them are going to run past you."

*Gosh, thanks, Coach.*

But his being frank with me helped. I knew what to expect. And he helped me to realize that everyone there was having the same thoughts about themselves. The key words there are *about themselves*. No one was thinking about me but *me*. And I could control that narrative.

I learned that weekend that I *do* belong at races like the World Championships, and it's not because I'm fast. (Remember, I'm not.)

I believe we fit into the areas where we want to be. I want to be around triathletes. And that's where I was at. I want to be around a community of people with a common goal. That's where I was at. I want to be around the cheering and the words of affirmation. And that's where I was at.

At first, I couldn't see the things that made me fit in with them, or that made me as good as them and as worthy of being there as them. Just because we might have different abilities doesn't make any group better than another. If we're around the right people, we're going to have something in common, no matter what our abilities are. That will unite us.

Acceptance is knowing that we all have commonalities. And it's also accepting that I don't have to be like somebody else to be me. Once you reach acceptance of these truths, it makes the fear of fitting in easier to set aside.

### Everyone's looking at me in my swimsuit!

No, they're not.

Really. They're thinking that *you* are looking at *them*!

But just because this is true doesn't make it any easier for someone worried about how their body looks in a swimsuit or tri kit, especially if they've experienced body shaming.

In my experience, both women and men are vulnerable to having these feelings, and at least some of the insecurity comes from the images that often portray our sport. Professional athletes have been the ones commonly shown in photographs, so that creates an expectation – even though triathletes come in all sizes and shapes. Only recently have I noticed media and marketing around triathlon starting to reflect the true diversity in our sport, including body diversity.

For some people, this is a sincerely difficult and distressing aspect of the sport, and I'd like to tell them, "You're creating your own gremlins in your mind, and they are limiting you." But I know body shaming is a real thing, and it leaves more damage than a Gremlin fed after midnight.

*Morgon Latimore*

So I'm more likely to tell someone who is scared of wearing a swimsuit, cycling tights, or tri kit: "Who you are, what you look like, or what size you are doesn't define what kind of athlete you can be. You have the choice to sculpt your mind and body in any way, shape, or form you choose." Or not at all.

I meet athletes who have body insecurity with compassion, empathy, and sensitivity, and I create an environment where it's safe to throw out the artificial standard that they've been comparing themselves to. Getting over body insecurity can take a long time, though, and sometimes it takes a trained professional. When expert help is needed, I urge you to get it.

**I am too old for this.**

Think back to the adults you knew when you were a kid. Were they out doing triathlons? Not likely. In their spare time, they were probably doing family stuff or gardening or working on their cars. Extreme sports like triathlon are really in their first generation, so role models are few.

I like to point out exceptions, like the 98-year-old woman who would come to a spin class I taught. Or one of my past coaches, who is in his 70s. Health and fitness as a lifestyle is new to a lot of adults, though, and that can be scary. That's where the fear of being "too old to tri" comes from.

The reality is, though, that most days as you get older, you aren't slowing down. You're getting faster, stronger, wiser. Your muscles mature, and for a long while, that's a great thing.

Mother Nature is Mother Nature, though, so at a certain point, everything starts decreasing, and it's important to know that age is not what defines you – it only tells you how ripe you are! You can choose to look at the number as a measurement of fragility, or you can look at it as your resilience score.

If you've made it to where things start trending downhill, well, there are plenty of others who were unable to reach the downslope and are not here. What are you going to do? Get out there and TRI.

**I might die doing this.**

Let's acknowledge one truth: You never know when you're going to have your first heart attack. It could happen when you're in the middle of your first triathlon, or it could happen when you're fixing dinner one night for your family. If this is one of your fears, or if you have a medical condition that might affect your training or performance, go see your doctor. Get a thorough physical and the assurance that you are healthy enough to train and compete.

Make sure you are honest with your physician. They base their assessments on information you provide. Don't leave anything out, and be sure to ask these questions: What can I do? How do I do it correctly? How often should I do it? What should I not do? What pain is too much?

The answers to these questions will give you and your coach guidelines to create something that is beneficial to your success and your health.

After that, if actual death is still a fear, it's time to get creative. If your fear stems from overexerting yourself and the discomfort that can come from an accelerated heart rate, skip the sprints and speed work and concentrate on aerobic or tempo-based workouts. That's just one suggestion, but the idea is to concentrate on what you can do successfully (both mentally and physically) and build up from there.

Everything that we've covered in this chapter about fear is about how we perceive ourselves and what we choose to allow into our minds and our hearts. When we let the good in, we let in the perseverance, the grit, and the creativity. We can reflect positively on what we have accomplished, instead of what we are afraid to try.

What makes people stronger is not always muscles or how fast they are. It is how strong their heart is and how strong their mind is to push through hard things like fear.

# CHAPTER 8
## GOAL-SETTING

**Core value:** Perseverance

**Growth quote:** "If you don't know where you are going, you will never get there."

**Call to action:** Use the acronym SMART (Specific, Measurable, Achievable, Realistic, and Timely) to set one goal for the day.

**Mantra:** Idea + Direction = Destination

Goal-setting is a ginormous part of every triathlete's success, and every goal must have a plan.

If you look at most achievements in life, there's some level of planning, because that's the fastest and most efficient way to get to where you want to be, whether it is going on a trip, graduating from college, getting a new job, or completing a triathlon. People who don't accomplish things don't plan.

I can't tell you how many times I've been approached by an athlete, and they tell me, "I want to do such-and-such race."

"OK," I'll say. "How do we do that?"

And the answer almost always is, "I don't know." It's like when they envision a goal, they expect it to just magically happen.

But that's not how life is, and creating a plan toward a goal is like paving the road to your destination. In triathlon, that looks like small, individual successes in each discipline's race strategy, nutrition, recovery, stretching ... all the pieces that add up to the whole. There might be 100 mini goals and accomplishments on the way to the big goals you set for yourself.

This is one of those skills, like many other ones in this book, that transcends sport. The scale of planning and goal-setting and achievement is bigger than triathlon. Once you learn that you can make something happen by doing small, obtainable things, the process can be applied to all areas of life. (I once read a story about a man who ate a bicycle. Why? Who knows? But how? By cutting it down into small, digestible bites. So, see? This can be applied to literally anything – but I don't recommend you eat your bike.)

In the triathlon world, any big goal, whether it's an Ironman or Ultra or a neighborhood sprint tri, can and should be broken into small, digestible bites. The overall race and all three disciplines can be overwhelming, but if you say, "Today, I'm just going to swim." And the next day, you say, "Today, I'm going to put the swim with the bike." Before long, you will build into and even beyond your goal. You will be ready well before race day, and that's the point. You will have deposited all the fitness into your fitness bank, and it will be time to cash out.

Planning can take time, so don't be impatient. In the beginning, you might know nothing, but it will snowball if you first learn what it takes for the swim, then the bike, then the run, then the recovery. It might take six months or more to learn how to put the whole thing together. People don't always like the process. They want to rush it.

But look at the military. Look at big corporations. They have quarterly goals, yearly goals, and five- and 10-year projections. As big operations like these march toward a goal, there are always small steps along the way.

The other thing to do is to reverse-engineer your goal, meaning to work backward from it. Ask yourself questions. What are the steps, what are the tools, what is the system that you need to put in place? You might have to write the answers down, and then, you have to take care of one little chunk at a time.

So, yes, there's more to it than just planning. You have to take action, too. A friend once told me, and I've heard it elsewhere since, "A dream without action is just an illusion." This is where and how your training comes into play, and how many of the other things we've covered in this book, like motivation and self-belief, kick in. Those factors help put plans in action.

Will it be easy? No. Will it be challenging? Yes. And that's the point. Growth comes from friction. Growth comes from learning something new. The ability to set goals is the ability to continue to grow. Goals every day

*Dion Cunningham*

create who we become tomorrow.

A lot of people come into triathlon with long-shot goals like Ironman or another endurance contest. That's OK for some people. They need a concrete goal to keep going. But for others, that can be too much, and it can become overwhelming or intimidating. For them, I say, "Let's just prepare your body and hit some milestones before you sign up for something."

Both approaches work, and both end up requiring small steps. If you already know how to swim, bike, and run, you need to plan how you'll put it all together. But I've had some athletes come to me after signing up for a race, but they don't know how to swim, yet. For people like them, there are things that need to be learned before we can even begin to implement a plan.

Even athletes who are physically strong will find benefits to approaching triathlon in little bits at a time. I have an athlete, Dion, who is a beast. He's in his 30s, and he was already a multisport athlete when we met, but he'd never trained for a triathlon.

Dion is a professional musician, so he's used to living with his sights set on an end goal, his performances. "When you know you're going to be on stage in five weeks ... you do everything it takes to be ready for that," he points out, and transferring that way of thinking to triathlon "was kind of a natural progression."

But since Dion got started in the sport during the Covid-19 pandemic, there were lots of disruptions to his plans.

We spent a long time with no race on the horizon, a situation perhaps forced by the pandemic, but it was good for Dion because he needed to work on smaller, fundamental things, like consistency, transitions, and nutrition, to achieve the bigger goals he had for himself.

Along the way though, we needed to do something competitive to keep things interesting, even if he had only himself to compete against. So we incorporated time trial days into his workout plan, something he says was particularly helpful to him.

"Setting those moments, those goals, so that I could see how I was progressing really helped me to get through the days where we just kind of sludged through longer workouts," Dion recalls.

The time trials "kept me honest," he elaborated, and provided a way to measure his progress, even without an official event to train for or enter.

Dion also set specific goals for his bike and to run under a six-minute mile. He's still working on them. "It can be frustrating to not hit the goal," he says, "but that's part of it. ... I've learned that you never really miss a goal, but sometimes you miss a deadline."

Sometimes, a deadline is missed through no fault of your own, be it a big detour like a pandemic, or something small. Dion has some advice for when you are forced off course:

"Miss a goal? Just set another one," he states. "Nothing is ever wasted in preparation to achieve a goal.

The person that you became in preparation for the goal is not the same person that began at the start of the goal. And so, I would say, you have to celebrate and also recognize that and continue to grow and develop into the new version of yourself.

"Goals are not necessarily about achieving or not achieving, but they're also about character development, and that's what this life is about. Life isn't so much about accomplishments. Life is also about what you overcome. And the most important person you overcome is yourself and the limitations you put on yourself."

With that outlook and attitude, it's no surprise that Dion has a true success story. At some point in his pandemic training, in the middle of long, lonely workouts, occasional time trials, nutrition education, and living a triathlete lifestyle, Dion asked me, "Do you think I could do a half Ironman?"

"Yeah, Bro," I told him. "You're totally ready to do that."

And he crushed it. He went under six hours in that half Ironman — his first race ever.

# CHAPTER 9
## DIVERSITY AND INCLUSION

**Core value:** Voice

**Growth quote**: "If we do it alone, it will never truly be done."

**Call to action:** Read one book about a culture other than your own.

**Mantra:** We are one.

Where I come from, most kids don't know what triathlon even is, let alone know anything about swim jammers or bike tights, nor do they ever even desire to run farther than a block. These things are just not prevalent in urban communities.

I was in high school when I first learned about triathlon. I saw the Ironman World Championship on TV one day when I was at my grandmother's house. It's funny what impressed my teenage self. I remember the race being sponsored by a beer company, for one thing, and I remember the people. Old, young, disabled.... *All these different people*! I remember thinking, *What is this crazy sport?*

Ironman knows how to turn up the volume on inspiration, and I remember getting emotional hearing the athletes' stories. I was amazed at the distances, too. I was the type of kid who would miss the bus on purpose, just so I could walk or run to school. So since that day seeing the Ironman on TV, I have wanted to be part of the triathlon world.

But I faced barriers, among them that I knew no one who did triathlons, so belief in myself that I could be a triathlete was low. Plus, I couldn't afford a bike, and I couldn't swim. Where I was from, people waded in the water, but no one swam.

The desire stuck with me, though. When I joined the Marine Corps, I learned to swim, and I bought my first bike at Walmart. I remember thinking I was something big – I spent $150 on that bike!

I was making the right steps, but no matter who I talked to about triathlon or endurance sports, that person didn't look like me. They didn't talk like me. They didn't act like me. I found myself wondering deep down, *Is this even for me?* I had seen so many different types of people on that Ironman broadcast, but at the local level when I was getting started in 2013, the diversity wasn't there. But since I am the type of person who likes to do things that are sometimes taboo, I kept showing up anyway.

I wasn't totally alone, though. There was at least one other Black guy doing triathlon in Southern California in those days. We'd see each other occasionally and joke, "Hey, man. You know only one of us can be at this race at a time!" At least once, my wife saw him on the course, and she started cheering wildly, "Go, Morgon, go!" only to realize he wasn't me when he ran by.

(And his fans and friends sometimes got me confused for him, too.)

I can laugh about that because even though being Black at a triathlon was lonely, I never felt ostracized or discriminated against. I never felt like I didn't belong. Way before anyone was talking about diversity and inclusion like they are today, I felt welcomed in the triathlon community. Nobody seemed to care what color I was or where I was from. They cared that I wanted to be healthy. They cared that I wanted to achieve something bigger than I ever had before.

I don't pretend that triathlon is without controversy when it comes to issues of race, diversity, access and inclusion. Every industry has work to do. We, as individuals, do too.

A woman once told me about going to the pool to swim with other triathletes, but when she saw she was the only Black woman there, she turned around and left. I told her, "If you want something to be more diverse, you can't be the one to leave. How are we ever going to start something, if every time we're the only one, we leave?"

It made me think back to my early days in triathlon, when I questioned, *Is this even for me? Am I supposed to be here?*

The answer to that is "Yes!" There has to be ground

*Morgon Latimore*

laid for everyone who comes after us.

If we exclude ourselves, then we'll never get the freedoms that we deserve. If we don't challenge racism, it will never change. If we don't challenge the status quo – the 60% Caucasian males in triathlon – it'll never change. We have to be the change that we seek.

So if you want to be a part of something, if you want to have a voice, then you have to interject yourself where needed, not just for yourself, but so other people can feel comfortable when they come along.

One day recently at the pool, I noticed three Black boys watching me swim. They were probably between 5 and 9 years old. I could feel their eyes on me, seeing me flip turn and keep going – when I swim, I don't stop – and I thought, *I didn't have anything like this when I was their age*.

I want to be that example, and we need more people to do that, too. That means if you're heavy-set, or a woman, or LGBTQ+, or whatever you are, you can't be afraid to get out there and be the first to break the mold, so others behind you can experience the joy of being within a community like triathlon.

You might feel like you don't belong, but you can become a representative of positivity, resilience, and grit, and then you represent not only your people, but also acts of enthusiasm for the sport. Triathlon looks at how you can be better, no matter what color you are.

So what's the practical first step when you find yourself feeling insecure, wondering if, where, or how you fit into the triathlon space?

Do it, anyway.

It's really that simple. Don't run away. Stop worrying about things that don't matter, and just enjoy yourself. Get out there and express yourself. Get out there and inspire other people to do hard things. Think to yourself, *Does it even matter if they think I belong here or not? Nope, because I'm here right now.*

Representation matters, and that means someone has to go first. So if you get the opportunity to be first, go for it!

What about the other barriers to entry and participation, like economic hurdles or a lack of exposure? If you have an opportunity to chip away at these barriers, knock them down. Can you buy a kid some running shoes? What about a bike? Or how about buying and donating a few pairs of goggles?

Or – seriously – ask for your pool's lost-and-found goggle stash and pull out a few pairs for kids who will appreciate them. Along the same lines, you can organize a bike drive to collect wheels for people who need them. I know plenty of adults who can't ride a bike. Why? Because they were never given the opportunity to learn.

You can give that opportunity, no matter what color you are. But at the end of the day, it's representation that truly facilitates people's thinking. When someone sees someone who looks like them, they can't help but think, *He's just like me. He understands me.*

I like the way Sika Henry, the first African American female professional triathlete, once put it: "Awareness and image can be incredibly impactful. Sometimes just seeing that something is possible can have a domino effect."

Do I wish I'd had a role model back when I first saw the Ironman World Championship on my grandmother's TV set? Of course, I do. I'm also grateful that the spark lasted until I was an adult and found my place in the triathlon community, which felt welcoming to me.

In the time since I started in triathlon, I've seen a lot of growth both in the sport and in society, in general, about the importance of representation in sport and in life. On the big stage, the Black community has woken up all types of people, including myself. Growing up, like a lot of kids, I was in a bubble. Then I went into the Marine Corps, which has to be one of the most diverse organizations on the planet, and I put myself into another bubble – one that deflected stupidity and ignorance. So it wasn't until I was older that I started to see things for what they are.

As I've talked to other Black triathletes in recent years, I've learned about some of the difficulties they've had in the sport – trials that mirror real-world problems around discrimination and equality. It's made me question my own experience and realize that I faced more pushback and opposition than I realized at the time. I missed it because I was so focused on my training and performance, but the conversation is more front-facing now, so I'm learning. I see it now: *Yeah, I sometimes got those looks, too.*

Still, if I focused on all the wrongs and negativity in my life, I would never be able to live a life of joy and happiness. We have to focus on things that we can do better – to teach, inspire, and create a better, more inclusive, and more diverse community.

Change will come, but we need to be that change. If we want hope, we have to be hopeful. If we want to see courage, we have to be courageous. And if we can't reflect that, we can't expect change to happen. We can't be mad when we're not accepted in spaces if we're not doing the work to be accepted.

So keep showing up. We all have equal responsibility to make change happen.

# CHAPTER 10
## DROPPING THE EGO TO BECOME A BETTER TRIATHLETE

**Core values:** Peace, vulnerability, mindfulness

**Growth quote:** "Letting go of what you think you need will attract the people and things that are meant for you."

**Call to action:** For 5-10 minutes a day, meditate on accepting what is and not trying to control things you can't control.

**Mantra:** Just let go.

This one's for the guys: Stop hiding behind your ego.

I've often wondered why it has been a challenge to coach some male athletes. I always felt like they have a wall up, and my holistic approach to coaching was maybe not a good fit for men who stand behind their egos and masculinity.

So I committed myself to learning more about men and how they are built emotionally and mentally.

I learned so much about myself in the process, and

I realized that I have suffered from depression for most of my life. Learning this has been so freeing. It also has challenged who I thought I was and helped me realize my own truth.

Also, it helped me understand that most male athletes lack vulnerability due to social norms that have been instilled in us for years. It saddens me to learn that we think embracing ego over emotional growth is what real men do, especially in the endurance sports culture.

I talk about this with my athletes because it's one of the things in my own life that I've not gotten to express much. The 'hood where I grew up and the Marine Corps are both survival environments where vulnerability isn't typically allowed.

But I studied this, and I saw that the best coaches and leaders in history have embraced their emotions and have used them to pave the way for the masses that they lead. As athletes, this is an area that many overlook in their athletic growth. And with that, we are left wanting, feeling like something is missing.

If training more helps you to podium or achieve that next personal record, why not also strengthen your mental and emotional resolve to supercharge your performance and overcome those mental and emotional gremlins that you have been fighting for years?

Think about it. You wouldn't ever just train one side of your body. You'd never say, "I'm only going to swim with my left arm," when your right arm is just as able and strong.

When you leave out the emotional side of things, it's like choosing to not use all that you have.

Men, being introspective and accepting our emotions is hard because it goes against all we have been told/taught our entire lives, but it's necessary for continued growth. It will not only make us better athletes, but it will also make us better fathers, husbands, brothers, and sons.

It's also going to help you push through those hard, hard workouts when you want to give up. For me, when I get to that hard place, I think about my brother or my grandmother, and I get an extra boost. If they were here in front of me, I'd give them 100 percent, so I paint a picture in my mind that they are really here. And I give them everything.

How can you tell when you are making choices based on your ego? It's when you are doing what you think society expects of you, so you can impress whoever you think is paying attention. (Guess what? They're not.) For men, though, that often means going overboard on the physical side of things.

But when you focus just on the physical side, and you push-push-push, you will break, and the walls come tumbling down because you don't have the scaffolding on the mental and emotional sides.

That's why you see a lot of men within the sport sink into a big depression when they DNF or don't hit a mark or don't make a cutoff. And then they might get stuck because society has told men to deal with their shit on their own. Our egos keep us from asking for help, and that compounds issues.

If you take anything away from this book, I hope it's that you can lean on the triathlon community.

And those of us in a good place need to offer our help to others. When we see someone suffering, we need to reach out to them and say things like, "Hey, I've been through the same thing."

"I've been through a DNF."

"I've had hard times in my relationship."

"I've had a hard time with injuries."

"You know, yeah, I don't have the greatest gear, either."

When you see someone struggling, and you know their body is already fatigued from training, it can get dark. Have the tough conversations. Doing so will help not only the men, but the women, too. The worst thing you can do is say nothing.

# CHAPTER 11
## OVERCOMING – AND WELCOMING – DARK MOMENTS

**Core value:** Vulnerability

---

**Growth quote:** "We have prepared our whole lives for one moment."

---

**Call to action**: Develop a plan to deal with dark moments in training, racing, and life. This way you are proactive, not reactive.

---

**Mantra**: I am the light in the darkness.

It's the second day of Ultraman Florida that'll get you.

The epic endurance race covers three days of grueling competition. The first has a 6.2-mile swim and a near-century bike ride. Day 2 is all on the bike – 171 miles through central Florida. A double marathon rounds out Day 3. All of it is daunting and excruciating, but it's those 171 miles on the second day that'll doom you. Boy, can I tell you about it.

In 2018, I raced Ultraman Florida. The first day went fine. It was challenging, but I never had that feeling like the buoys were moving away from me. Plus, the bike after the swim felt great.

Day 2 was a completely different story. I'm not a weak cyclist, but I found myself in the back of the pack almost immediately. I was so far back that I was trading places for the last spot with a young woman who ended up not finishing that day.

I tried to not let it bother me. *Ride your own race, Morgon,* I told myself. *There are 171 miles to go.*

My training for this race had been questioned. My coach was inexperienced, and my preparation was unconventional. My coach had been told that I would never finish because he had never before trained anyone for Ultraman. Even though both he and I knew that I was well-trained and had the grit to complete anything, doubts began to surface once I started to feel like junk.

As I dragged, people got concerned. My energy level was low. My power was low. My speed was low. My crew approached me on the course. "Are you alright?" they asked.

At about 120 miles in, I pulled off for a pit stop. Usually, I wouldn't get off my bike. It would be a grab-and-go nutrition break. But this time, I got off, and my crew asked how I was feeling, I said, "It is what it is."

People who know me know that I'm never like that. My crew knew something was way, way wrong.

But I didn't see it, and I kept going. When you're in a

dark moment like that, you don't see anything else. You don't see the light at the end of the tunnel. You don't see a way out. You don't see a solution. You just know you're going through some shit, and you think you're there by yourself, and no one understands you.

As I pedaled, I fantasized about quitting – not only whether I would quit, but how. The negativity was not "normal Morgon," and questions ran through my brain: *Why are you even here? Do you even deserve to be here?*

*I've never quit before,* I thought, and I started planning it out in my head – what I was going to say, what I'd put on social media, who I'd apologize to and how.

*Or maybe I shouldn't tell anyone*, I countered with myself. *Or maybe I should just keep riding, even if I don't make the 12-hour cutoff.*

There was no way to win this internal debate, and there was no way to win the race while it was going on. I was in a dark place.

Desperate for help, my crew called my nutritionist, and it was like dialing a lifeline on "Who Wants to Be a Millionaire."

"Give him a banana," my nutritionist said.

That banana changed the course of everything. My mood switched. I started making jokes and cheering. The change wasn't just on the outside. It was within. I was rejuvenated.

I started to think clearly, strategizing the hills,

deciding when to ride conservatively, willing myself to stay focused, and pushing to turn up the tempo. *Stop worrying about pacing and do what you do best and ride*, I told myself.

I started catching people. And passing them.

What a 180 – all from a banana! Or was it only the banana, after all?

Surely, the banana provided the fuel to make the change. The chemicals in my brain and body were clearly out of whack that day, and I'll forever turn to nutrition and hydration first, if I ever find myself in a similar dark place again. It's crazy how something seemingly so small can make such a drastic difference. Like, when there were only 10-15 miles to go that day, that's when I felt like I'd finally found my groove.

But once things were kickstarted by the banana, the real turnaround came because I realized the pain I was in was temporary. Knowing this provided the mental energy I needed to be reinvigorated.

What I've learned since then is that we all have these dark moments. I've had many more than just this Ultraman experience. I've had them being deployed in Afghanistan, being away from my family, getting shot at, rocketed. I've had them in my professional life. My marriage. And, of course, in triathlon.

These things happen because you're pushing the limits. Your body's never been pushed like that before, so it's telling you, "You ain't ready for this! This is not safe!"

But you can override this, and every time you override a dark moment, it prepares you for the next one, and it builds on your ability to persevere and to have grit.

As uncomfortable as they are, I believe dark moments like these are a main reason why many people do triathlon in the first place.

Dark moments let you relive experiences in your life and come out with clarity. They bring very emotional, negative experiences to you, but they also give you the ability to address them. When you are so fatigued that a dark moment comes upon you, it's almost like drinking alcohol. Your guard comes down. There's no security for your feelings, and your body doesn't have the energy to both move forward and keep you ostracized from your emotions.

So it picks one, and usually the fitness side wins out. You might power through that ride or run, but the walls and barriers surrounding the emotions and experiences you've been burying will come open. I know this firsthand.

My younger brother was murdered by being shot in the face. We grew up in the 'hood, and while I made it out, my brother got sucked in by drugs and violence. He wasn't the only person I knew to end up dead like this, but when it's your little brother, it's different. I had tried to protect him my whole life.

I remember getting the call after he'd been shot, and I went home. I felt like I needed to be my mom's rock. She had just lost a child.

I never cried.

For years, I would take walks, and I would try to make myself cry. I would try to make myself feel. But I couldn't. I didn't know what to do, and when they wanted to send me home from work, I was, like, "No. I want to stay here. I don't want to be by myself."

I never grieved.

Then one day, I was doing an eight-hour ride on a trainer. (That's a long day that could make anyone cry.) This workout tapped into every vulnerable place in my body and mind.

To fight boredom, I was watching a movie, something that had two brothers in it, and one of them was going into space or something, and the other brother had to make some sort of sacrifice for this to happen. The storyline doesn't really matter.

What counts is that I just absolutely lost it. In my physical exhaustion, the walls I'd kept up around my brother's death suddenly came crumbling down.

"What's wrong?" my wife asked when she saw me off my bike, sweaty and sobbing. I could barely speak. I just kept saying that I missed him. And I was sorry. I'll probably feel this way forever, and as awful as it is to feel such loss, I'm so grateful to finally feel it at all.

Dark moments are going to happen. I prepare my athletes for them, and at a certain level, dark moments can even be welcomed. They expose your deepest vulnerabilities, and when you overcome something like that, it creates a degree of strength most people didn't know they were capable of. It's that inner strength that makes you a better triathlete in the long term.

One of my athletes, Sherri, is exceptional when it comes to using dark moments to her advantage and to the advantage of others. She's in a good place now, but she's had to process a lot of dark moments in her life.

Sherri really feels things – she describes herself as an empath – and sometimes those feelings can be negative and almost paralyzing to her. She's had years of heartbreak over mystery medical issues and, understandably, she's had accompanying roller-coaster emotions. In the throes of a triathlon season, this combination can make it hard for her to be her own cheerleader.

We all need to be our own biggest fans, but Sherri struggles with this. "I can give the best advice and motivation in the world. But, man, I suck at doing it for myself," she explains.

"If your heart and soul are not feeling the positivity that you need, it can really break you, because this is such a mental sport that we do," Sherri says. "We all have our own battles. We all have highs and lows."

So what are some practical ways to deal with dark moments? Sherri finds strength in the camaraderie of the triathlon community. (Shout out to Sherri's tribe!)

"It's honestly what keeps me moving," she adds. "My hope is that I can be a part of helping others, so that I can

*Sherri Bond*

help them to keep moving, too. It really does something in my heart. It just brings so much joy."

By mentoring other triathletes, Sherri can push past her own dark moments. When her mentees feel the thrills the sport can bring, she, by extension and empathy, feels them, too.

"Even the weak moments can be turned into something strong," she says. "Yes, it's OK to have these dark moments, but it's what you do with those dark moments that matters. ... Figure out how to make it better. Figure out that you aren't alone."

Here are some more practical, real-life steps to pushing through and making the most of a dark moment:

Let yourself feel. Don't deny that you're fatigued or that something is wrong. If you block out emotions and realities like that, when the dam finally breaks – and it will – you won't be prepared. You've got to feel it to learn how to handle it. You can also use those emotions to your advantage. Let them come in. Now, if I bring the emotions about my brother with me on a bike or a run, it's like having a superpower. Everything about my effort increases.

Accept that things are going to go wrong, and learn when it happens. Like, when I feel myself tanking now, I always make sure my hydration and nutrition are on point. And if that's all good, I need to ask myself, *What else is going on?* You don't want to be thinking, *I'm weak, why do I even do this? I quit.* Don't take the easy way out. Ask yourself, *How can I be better? Why is this happening to me now? What can I do to fix it?* Triage dark emotions in the moment.

At the end of the day, dark moments are part of what makes us all human, and it's worth it to use all of what you've got to become better at what you do. So even the dark times have a place on your triathlon journey. When they come, welcome them.

# CHAPTER 12
## HARMONY WITH THE WATER

**Core value:** Adventure

**Growth quote:** "Stop fighting what you can't control. Become one with what you seek to understand."

**Call to action:** Build your relationship with the water by spending one day a week just playing in it. Play Marco Polo, swim under water, or create an underwater world.

**Mantra:** Relax.

Whether it's a pool sprint, a meander in a murky lake, or a through-the-breakers-and-around-the-pier race with the fishes, no triathlon swim is the same. That's part of the beauty and attraction of triathlon swimming. You never know what you're going to get. Even the same course will vary year-to-year with weather conditions, environmental changes, the number of people swimming with you, and your own fitness and readiness to take all of that on.

At the same time, each swim shares at least two common traits. The first is that the swim part of triathlon is one of the largest barriers to participation in the sport. The second is that the incredible feeling of accomplishment that comes as a result of overcoming that barrier is so worth it.

I can't tell you how many times someone has said to me, "I'd love to do a triathlon, but I can't swim."

Really? Can't or won't? Can't or haven't tried? Most of the time, the person who can't swim has convinced themselves of their own inability by never having tried. The especially sad part of this is how many other life experiences are limited by the lack of swimming skills. I know people who have skipped family vacations that involve water, who don't enjoy their own backyard pools, and who have come to me in a panic ahead of a cruise, desperate to learn to swim, "just in case."

I know people who don't like to get their face wet in the shower, even.

I remember my own mother, who doesn't swim, visiting me in Southern California when I was stationed there. She said she wanted to go to the ocean. I thought (I don't know why) she wanted to go in the water. But she literally walked out to where the water was coming up on the sand, took off her shoes, stepped in for one second, and then said, "We can go now."

"Don't you want to hang out on the beach, Mom?" I asked her.

"Nope. I don't need to be here anymore," she said.

So for a lot of people, swimming and water in general represent a hurdle to true enjoyment of a lot of things. They are truly missing out. There's a good deal of research into how water is elemental to human existence, and about how being around it makes us feel better and be better. That explains why so many people are soothed by the presence of water or will pay extra for the ocean view cabin on their cruise ship, and how people who don't feel and know the tranquility of water are almost in a state against their own nature.

We talk a lot about how success in triathlon cascades into success in other areas in life. This is most applicable to the swim. When someone overcomes the inability to swim, it creates overarching confidence. Learn to swim, and now you can take scuba lessons. Learn to swim, and now you've got the confidence to rent the glass-bottomed kayak when you're on vacation in Hawaii. Learn to swim, and you can start fully living in ways you've never before.

When you're ready to learn to swim, the next question is, how? Lessons, of course, in the most practical sense are part of the picture, but there's more to it. You need a positive relationship with water in order to be comfortable, and that comes with the application of two things: time and play.

The more time you spend cultivating a relationship with water – or with anything, for that matter – the more comfortable you will be. With that comfort, there comes a level of respect and understanding. That's huge when it comes to water, because most of us think the more control you have over something, the better you know it.

Water is not made to be muscled, though. It is fluid, and when you go with its flow, not only will you learn to work with it, it will stop working against you.

OK, so what do you do with all this time you're going to spend in and with the water?

CANNONBALLLLLL!!!!!

That's right. Have fun. Once you learn the basics, or even as part of your time with an instructor, make time to play.

Jump in. Do some flips. See how far you can go underwater. Pick up pennies from the bottom of the pool. The psychological and emotional benefits of goofing off cannot be undervalued, and they go a long way toward building and maintaining your positive relationship with the water.

People don't or won't swim for lots of reasons, and so far, we've talked about the traditional nonswimmer – someone who has never learned. But what about people who know how to swim but who have had a bad experience in the water? What about the ones who know how to swim in a pool but who freak out in open water?

A bad experience in the water is a rational, trauma-based fear, and it can take years and professional help before a person is ready to swim again. A little help from friends can go a long way, too.

I once gave a swim clinic to a group of women triathletes, and one of them, Susan, had once been bitten by a shark. True story: As a child, she and her sister had been playing inside a protected area of a beach in South Africa. She was surprised by a sharp pain, and while all she remembers is screaming and running out of the water, it turns out that a small shark had wiggled through the swimming area's netting and taken a bite of her leg. She was 7 years old.

Now 60, Susan did become a pool swimmer, but she spent a lifetime never going past her shins in open water, which is an understandable response to her experience.

When she started doing triathlons a couple of years ago, she stuck to sprint tris that took place at swimming pools. *I'm never going to do one in the open water*, she told herself. *I don't want to go there. I don't need to. I've done what I wanted to do in the pool.*

But ...

"Once you join a tribe of women who are all doing all the different (kinds of) swimming, there's a feeling like a wanting for you to do it, as well – to keep up," she said. "I'm not even a competitive person, but that little bit that was there wanted to do it with everybody else."

And that's how Susan ended up at my swim workshop at a murky lake in North Carolina.

I've never worked with a swimmer who'd been bitten by a shark before. Sure, I've had plenty of athletes who are afraid of sharks, but when I heard Susan's story, I was like, *Oh, wow. This is for real this time.*

*Susan Traynor*

I was impressed with her courage, but I knew we had to take it slow. For Susan, this low-key approach was imperative.

"(Coach Morgon) made sure to know that there was no pressure," Susan remembers. "If you didn't even want to put your foot in, you didn't have to. There was nobody, saying, 'Come on, now. Come on, we're all here. Come on.' There was none of that. It was just totally up to me."

Peer pressure was not going to work for Susan. "I have to go in on my own volition," she says.

Susan and two other women decided to walk in – baby steps – together, and I told them, "If you want to come out, just come out."

Before they really realized it, they were in waist-deep water, and they stayed there for a minute, just bobbing around.

"Do you want to swim out to the buoy?" I asked them after a while, and they did.

The women took a break at the buoy, catching their breath that was quick from adrenaline and exercise. And then they came back to the shoreline.

For Susan, it was a thrilling breakthrough, yet her truthful assessment is that it "wasn't all unicorns and dancing fairies."

"I was nervous," she recalled. "And I worried about things touching my leg. I knew there were muskrats that lived in that lake, and I was just trying to not think about them touching me.

"I knew I could have gone farther," she says, "but for that day, it was enough. I had broken the seal, and it was a big, big step in my swimming career."

A few weeks later, Susan's family visited friends who had a lake house. She jumped in the water and swam with them. "On the social side of things, it was fantastic," she says. Soon, too, she signed up for an open water, three-mile river swim.

The swim organizers drove the participants upriver, so they could swim with the current back to their belongings and their cars. "On the way to the put-in point, I was thinking, *I'm probably not going to do it*, and then, I was like, *But I don't know how I'm going to get back! I don't have any shoes!*"

Susan then remembered a piece of advice from the swim clinic – when you're nervous about something, tell someone.

"I told the kayakers who were accompanying us that I was nervous, and that it would take a little for me to get my breathing under control, and they said, 'Absolutely. We'll keep an eye on you. No problem.'

"And I had a blast!"

Susan's advice to anyone apprehensive about the water is to get support.

"Going to that clinic was probably the best thing I did," she says. "I found someone who didn't dismiss my fear. If somebody is actually listening to you and listening to your fear, it helps. Because you're not really crazy, but it can feel that way sometimes."

# CHAPTER 13
## FAMILY FIRST/DEALING WITH GUILT

**Core values:** Voice, community, value

**Growth quote:** "Never feel guilty about self-care, but never forget about those that care about you."

**Call to action:** When your family needs you, make sure you choose them over training or racing. The keyword here is *needs*.

**Mantra:** Family first, always and forever.

Many coaches don't think about athletes as people. They think about them as athletes only, and you'll only hear them talking about the training, the nutrition, the preparation, the recovery – all the ingredients of a triathlete, except the person!

All that talk can add up to a lot of stress on the athlete, especially those who have families. Because how is someone supposed to train, eat right, recover and rest when they also have to shop and otherwise show up for the important people in their lives?

It can be too much, and one of my athletes, Tiffany, a

*Tiffany Ring*

wife, mother, and school counselor, may have put it best when she told me: "I want to do these races, but I feel so guilty being gone all day!"

Wow. Guilt is a heavy feeling. Isn't this supposed to be fun? Why should anyone spend their precious free time on anything that makes them feel guilty?

Her confession struck me and made me realize how important it is to recognize that people have things going on in their lives. "What can I do to help?" I asked her. "Let me know what else you have going on, and I'll put that as the top priority. I will build everything around that."

For Tiffany, that meant including her family in her workouts some days, and not working out at all on some others. I never wanted her to look back on triathlon and think, *Triathlon took so much away from me*. I wanted her to be able to think, *Triathlon enhanced my life*.

Putting family first works for Tiffany. The guilt is less (no mom is ever totally without guilt, right?), and she recently did a 70.3 race with a PR on the run and bike. She's proof that piling on the training at the expense of other things isn't the only way.

"I live with it," Tiffany says. "I still have that guilt of *Oh wait. I'm spending three hours of my day training, and I'm not taking care of my home, my husband....* Even though he's very independent and very supportive, I still have that inner guilt. It's just how I was raised."

Tiffany believes more women than men face this conflict, especially women of her generation.

*Jason Kwok*

"I have to constantly remind myself that it's OK to do something for me. And that doing something good for me is actually helping my family. I'm giving my kids a role model of what they can be like in their 40s, to constantly try to grow as a person."

Another of my athletes, Jason, has always been a family-first thinker. From the get-go, he trained no more than five days a week, and no more than 45 minutes at a time. Forty-five minutes! What can anyone accomplish in such a short amount of time? Turns out, a lot.

Jason has trained for all distances and types of races, and never in all the years I've known him, has he worked out on the weekend. Yet he still performs, he still PRs, and he still maintains his health.

Setting him up for success in a way that respected his commitment to his family really challenged me to change the way I coach. It also inspired me to rethink the way I live. I looked at the example he sets, and I learned.

Jason is very involved in his household, and he knows what he values most in life – his family – so he makes time for his wife, kids, mother, everyone. He wants to be healthy, and triathlon does that for him, but he knows his family relationship has to be healthy, too. This outlook has become huge for me as a coach, athlete, husband, and father, and when I encourage my athlete clients to adopt it as well, they thrive.

When we started, though, it was a gamble. I'd never trained anyone like Jason before, and he'd never been coached. Jason admits he was worried.

"I was worried that I wouldn't live up to his expectations," Jason says now. He thought that by working with a coach, I would be setting his goals and progress marks, and that put an unreasonable level of stress and pressure on him. It's like he was getting guilt from both sides.

Tiffany still struggles similarly. "If I shorten a run because I'm planning to go to the beach or spend time with my friends, or if I'm just tired one day and I don't want to do it, I feel like I'm letting my coach down and I'm letting myself down," she says.

Internal struggles like these might never completely resolve. They come from deeply-ingrained ideas about what it means to be an athlete. But after knowing and working with people like Jason and Tiffany, one of my goals as a coach has become to always work around what else is going on in a person's life – because wouldn't it be great to not have to deal with guilt, because guilt and resentment were prevented in the first place?

This is a departure from tradition in endurance sports, where it's not uncommon to hear of someone divorcing over the conflicts of training and competing versus a happy family life. The culture and message has for too long been, "I don't care about what your kids have going on this weekend. Figure it out."

And we wonder why people don't stay in the sport? We can't treat hobby-triathletes like professionals.

This mindset, though, is a two-way street. Athletes also have a responsibility to not let things go too far, get too serious, or overstretch both reasonable goals and expectations. Basically, if you're not making money from this, keep your head screwed on right.

You have to make your needs known and stick to your priorities, and then your coach should listen and adapt. That's a win for everyone.

Being with the ones we love invigorates us. It inspires us to do more, but when you go into something with a lot of stress from, say, not being around for your husband or from missing your kid's game, you're not going to be at your best for that bike ride anyway. You'll be distracted, and that's not how to be a better athlete.

Putting family at the forefront is how to stay happy in your triathlete journey, how to keep coming back for more, and how to alleviate stress, not add to it.

# CONCLUSION AND FURTHER READING

A triathlon is made up of three disciplines: swimming, biking, and running. (Four, if you count the recovery, which you know I do!)

But almost infinite disciplines make up an extraordinary triathlete.

In this book, we've taken a close look at many of those characteristics, skills, attributes, habits, and attitudes that help a triathlete be the most successful. As you find ways to implement the tips, advice, and mindset, you will uncover your triathlon superpowers and develop the systems and practices that work best for you.

Personal and athletic education is a forever journey, however, so if you've enjoyed this book and want more, please consider the resources listed below. They have all helped to shape my thinking and the way I live my life, and I recommend them highly.

*The Alchemist: A Fable About Following Your Dream* by Paulo Coelho (HarperOne, 2014)

*Atomic Habits: An Easy & Proven Way to Build Good Habits & Break Bad Ones* by James Clear (Avery, 2018)

*Daring Greatly: How the Courage to Be Vulnerable Transforms the Way We Live, Love, Parent, and Lead* by Brene Brown (Avery, 2015)

*You Are a Badass: How to Stop Doubting Your Greatness and Start Living an Awesome Life* by Jen Sincero (Running Press Adult, 2013)

*Grit: The Power of Passion and Perseverance* by Angela Duckworth (Scribner, 2018)

# ACKNOWLEDGMENTS

I am known as The Peoples Coach, and this book could not have been written without my people, namely and especially the athletes who bravely and honestly shared their stories for these pages: Patricia Howe, Barbara Ogle, Akila O'Grady, Ryan Anderson, Angela Jackson, Dion Cunningham, Sherri Bond, Tiffany Ring, Jason Kwok, and Susan Traynor. Thank you all.

# AUTHOR'S BIOGRAPHY

Coach Morgon Latimore is a U.S. Marine Corps veteran, author, personal trainer, and coach. He became an endurance coach more than 20 years ago because he felt athletes deserved more honesty and better communication, and he knew that athletes needed to be coached for who they are as individuals. Coach Morgon, known as The Peoples Coach, has completed 5Ks to 50-mile running races, multiple Ironman and Ironman 70.3 races, Ultraman, RAAM challenge, and many other endurance events.

Coach Morgon believes his success comes from seeing each athlete's abilities and showing them how to best move forward to accomplish their goals and dreams. He prides himself on building athlete-coach relationships that foster trust, resilience, and happiness. These things, along with his high level of technical skill and detailed knowledge in coaching, help him redefine athletes' possibilities.

Coach Morgon grew up in Kansas City and St. Louis, Missouri. He retired from the Marines in 2022 after 24 years of service. A dad to four girls, he lives in North Carolina with his wife and youngest daughter. He has written four books.

Looking to be coached by Coach Morgon, so that you can have the same success as the 300-plus athletes before you? Contact him at: Info@MorgonLatimore.com.

CPSIA information can be obtained
at www.ICGtesting.com
Printed in the USA
LVHW081349090422
715719LV00015B/544